IMPRINT
CLASSICS

GETTING

GOLD

The ABC of Prospecting in Australia

"Fossicker"

ETT IMPRINT

Exile Bay

This edition published by ETT IMPRINT, Exile Bay 2025

First published in Australia in 1931 by Robertson & Mullens

New edition with additional maps compiled by Tom Thompson
First ebook published by ETT Imprint in 2025

ISBN 978-1-923527-02-7 (pbk)
ISBN 978-1-923527-03-4 (ebk)

Design by Tom Thompson

Cover: The Author in action.

GETTING GOLD

AN A B C OF PROSPECTING IN AUSTRALIA

EXPLAINING IN SIMPLE, NON-
TECHNICAL LANGUAGE, THE
METHODS OF GETTING GOLD BY
MEANS OF PANNING, CRADLING,
PUDDLING, DOLLYING,
SLUICING, ETC.

BY

"FOSSICKER"

ROBERTSON & MULLENS LIMITED
MELBOURNE
1931

INTRODUCTION.

Of recent months there has grown up a large and insistent demand for a handy non-technical and reasonably priced handbook dealing with the subject of gold prospecting, or, as might be more truly termed, gold fossicking.

Hard times and dearth of employment, coupled with the prevailing note of depression, have served to create a "Gold sense" in the community. Every unemployed man or youth, indeed, every schoolboy about to leave the shelter of school life, has felt, or now feels, the call and thrill of the master lure, gold.

The numbers of intending prospectors and fossickers are large, but, as yet, apart from some help given by State Departments of Mines aided by small Government grants, little has been done to wield this vast quest for gold into a corporate, disciplined and well-guided entity.

The class of men offering are good types—good education, strong physique and a native determination and courage in turning to a new field for endeavour and, perchance, fortune, are the outstanding characteristics.

To the vast majority of these men, digging for gold is an unknown job, and it is for these amateur gold-winners that this little handbook has been written.

The field is large, a whole continent lies before us, its possibilities and potentialities but yet scarcely scratched, and the reward is great.

To the country, as well as to the individual, gold is the pressing need of the moment, and the time and energy spent in the search thereof might well prove a boon to the one and a blessing to the other.

CONTENTS.

ILLUSTRATIONS.

72 oz
found in the bank of a Creek at
Creswick by Harold Beer & J. Wescott
in 1931

Discovered in Grub Creek in late March 1931 in the blue grey clay, the gold nugget 6.5 x 2.5 x 1.5 inches in size, and actually 73 ounces, 6 pennyweight (2.2kg).

A 75-OUNCE NUGGET.

Students' Lucky Find.

BALLARAT, Tuesday.— It was reported to-day that James C. Westcott and Harold H. Beer, two youthful students of the School of Forestry, Creswick, were out walking on Sunday morning, and with the thought of gold in their minds, engaged in a little amateur fossicking with amazing luck. They unearthed a 75-oz. nugget, which was valued at the Bank of New South Wales at £389.

Apart from any consideration of the gold bonus, the find fired the imagination of the other students, who have joined together in parties to take up leases, upon which they will work in their spare time. The location of the find is being kept secret.

CHAPTER 1.

SETTING OUT.

The amateur, who is about to go forth on the quest for gold, might well be advised as a first step to make some enquiries at the Mines department. From the department's officials he can learn much that will prove of value—he will obtain suggestions as to the most likely districts where gold might be won, and also the best and handiest ways to set about its winning.

It must be borne in mind that the term "Prospector" is a much abused one. The true meaning of the term "to prospect" is to search for a definite show of minerals with a view to their further development by mining. In the old gold mining days a prospector, setting out, always made for new and virgin country in which to carry on his search for "a strike." Of latter years, however, the term "prospector" has been more usually applied to those who have gone out to "fossick" around old deserted workings and localities which have already, in many cases, yielded gold in previous years.

"To fossick," that is, to re-open old workings or to search for tracings of gold here and there which have been left behind by previous miners, is therefore, by far the more popular method adopted at the present time.

To the amateur "prospector," therefore, there are two distinct openings offered. The first is to strike out into new country, never before worked, and endeavour to make a strike or, as a second choice, to fossick around on creeks, dried up watercourses, rock formations, ridges or other workings which have been already worked and eventually abandoned.

In the first instance the chances may be that much time will be taken, and a vast amount of ground covered before any definite find results, whilst at the same instance, a strike once discovered might well prove very remunerative. On the other hand fossicking in country known to have yielded gold might possibly, from the very outset, yield wages, or what is generally termed "Tucker-money," with always the odd chance of discovering a pocket previously over-looked or a lead not fully exploited.

This latter method might with profit be adopted by the "new chum" prospector, as it would afford valuable experi-

ence and any show of colour, be it ever so slight, would en-
courage and lend fresh vigour to his quest.

The matter of equipment is an important one. Whilst
the details of the various tools needed will be dealt with in
a later chapter, a word or two concerning food supplies
might not be amiss at this stage. Whilst every embryo prospector realises that a tent and a frying pan are necessary
adjuncts to his existence "in the wilderness," but few rea-
lise that a matter of months might elapse before they have
been successful in finding even enough gold to purchase
provisions.

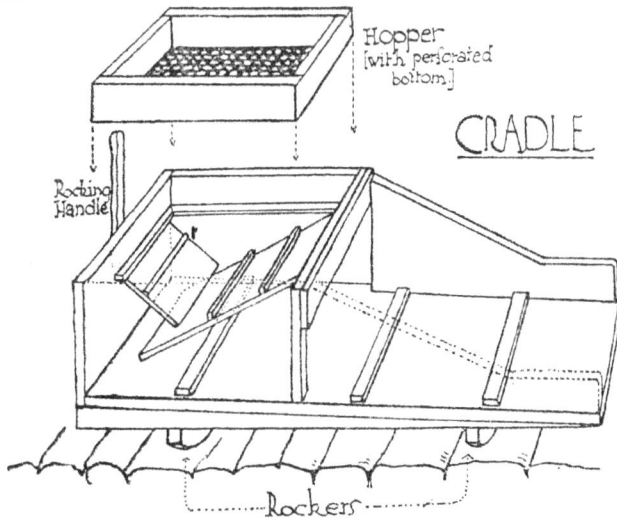

Therefore, it is recommended that before setting out
some attention be given to the necessity of providing and
arranging for a supply of foodstuffs to cover a period of,
say, three to six months. The subject matter of this pro-
visioning might be left to each individual to decide for himself. Suffice it to say that bacon, flour and coffee might be
regarded as staple items of diet amongst the supplies.

A technical knowledge of geology is not really essential,
although some working knowledge of rocks and rock deposits is desirable. As these remarks are addressed pri-
marily to those who, through force of circumstances not
under their control, have been compelled to take up prospecting as a possible means of livelihood, it will be advisable
to go somewhat into some detail concerning the simplest

methods of obtaining in the shortest possible time a little gold for the purpose of providing sustenance.

The working of shallow alluvial ground, as detailed in Chapter 2, with the aid of simple working tools, might well yield, in a very short period of time, a definite return to make secure the prospector's subsistence, coupled with the ever-present possibility of a stray nugget or patch of gold turning up.

The further suggestion made to those about to venture forth with no previous experience to guide them is that, if at all possible, a party of three or four be formed. Three men of this party may be new chums, and the fourth might have some previous knowledge, large or small, of actual prospecting.

The prospecting life is a healthy one, and one that must appeal to the average Australian who oft times has only to spend a day or two in the Bush country to feel quite at home there.

Certainly for a short time it may seem a hard life, but as days go on and the grip of the gold quest gets into one's veins, it holds a very distinct attraction and no small measure of charm and even pleasure.

CHAPTER 2.

THE FIELD OF OPERATIONS.

In searching for gold it is essential that all specimens of rock unearthed or broken off should be minutely examined. Every fragment of stone or slate, every chip of sandstone or rock might bear news to the prospector of the very thing he is most anxious to discover.

It will be well for the new-chum prospector to become acquainted with the appearance of various minerals and rock formations that he may encounter in his search for gold. If in Melbourne a visit to the Museum of Geological Survey in Spring Street will show him many things of value and interest.

A feature of this Museum is the fact that the specimens of quartz, rocks, etc., have been displayed in the correct order of their occurrence, that is to say, the oldest or Primary rocks are shown first. Then comes the second oldest or secondary and so on down to the most recent formations.

In prospecting for gold it is necessary that a careful and systematic search be made in all gullies, depressions, water courses, and other places where the never failing law of gravity deposits rubbish and rubble. It is particularly stressed that the search be thorough to the point of tediousness, every inch of ground being minutely observed and samplings of washings constantly being taken and examined.

If the gully or water course being worked is part of a field known to have already yielded gold, the colour of gold is almost certain to appear in the dish washings. Whether this happens or not, no attempt to move camp or to try elsewhere should be made until every reasonable chance of locating the gold deposit has been tried.

It must always be borne in mind that gold is not native to the newer formation of rocks. If some specimens are found in this new formation, then the possibilities are that it has been broken from some outcropping of old rock or strata and so washed to where it is discovered.

Should such stray specimens be discovered, the process known as loaming might be recommended. This consists of the operation of following up the clues offered in these detached portions, and eventually tracing them to the location at which they broke away from the parent lode. Loaming is a practice in prospecting frequently resorted to and oftentimes yields good results.

The true habitat of gold is in the old rocks, therefore, it may be necessary to penetrate several newer formations in order to locate the bedrock upon which to work. Occasionally, when searching for this bedrock, a false bottom may be discovered. This, in appearance and character, may well appear to be bedrock. It is necessary sometimes to go several feet deeper to ultimately discover the true bottom or bedrock.

It is a good idea when commencing the search to make a beginning at the lowest practicable point in the creek or gully and work gradually uphill. It must be remembered that if gold has been washed into the creek or watercourse, it will most likely be found in the centre of the stream, as the action of the water would naturally carry it there.

Special attention must be paid to the careful examination of all bars of rocks lying across the creek bed. The cracks and crevices in these bars are all possible harbourers of gold specks. These cracks and crevices must be scraped clean of any sand or clay or other substance which may be found to have lodged there. By careful washing these will disclose whether any gold has been washed down the creek.

When traces of gold are found in creek bottoms or in the bottoms of gullies, it must be borne in mind that these signs of gold are probably washings or breakaways from veins situated somewhere in the higher levels around, and consequently, the search must be directed towards these elevations.

Should further washings higher up the creek still show colors, a steady advance up the creek, together with constant sampling, must be undertaken. A sudden cessation of color in the washings would point to the fact that the gold had entered the creek at a point just below the position of the last washing. Having established this fact, search should be directed to the higher levels around, and a watch kept for any outcropping or break of rock formation.

In working up the creek bed, all bends or turns in the stream are worthy of special attention. Any gold carried down stream will naturally be caught up and deposited on the sides of cliffs or the rocky banks, where the stream takes a more or less sharp curve to right or left.

Caution must be displayed in not placing too much credence on the results, whether good or otherwise, of any one dish washing. In shallow alluvial work, one washing may give excellent results, whilst the next 50 dishes might not so much as show a color.

Should no show of gold whatsoever result from the dish washing of the surface dirt, it need not of necessity mean that there is no gold to be won in that particular area. In shallow ground, that is, where the silurian rocks are near to

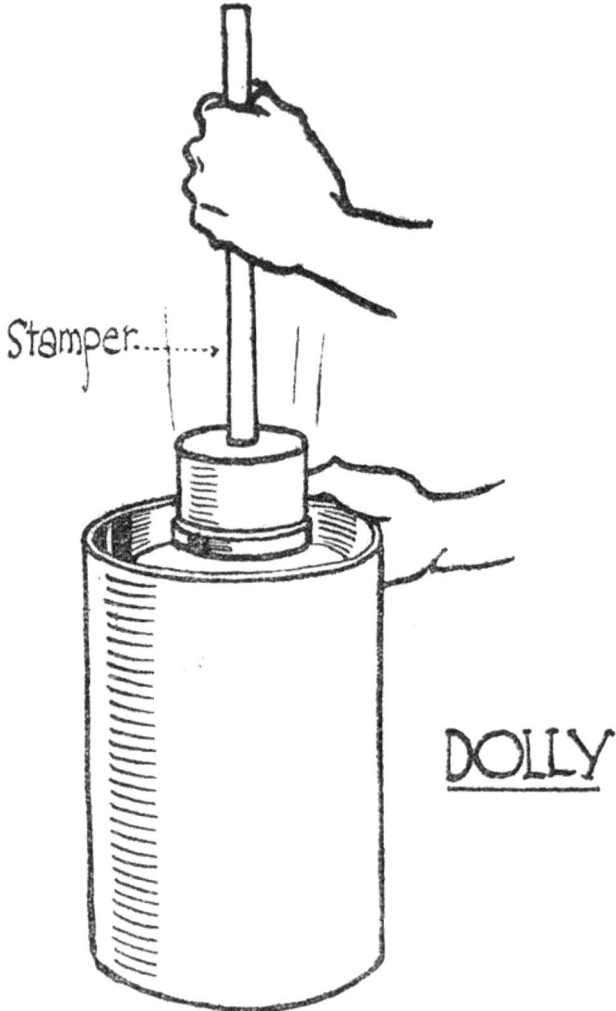

Stamper....⋯⋯→

DOLLY

the surface, it will prove an easy matter to sink to the bottom itself. A number of sinkings should be made, as it is quite possible to work to within a few inches of a likely vein, and yet pass on oblivious of its existence.

Ground which has been worked and re-worked, such as that at Ballarat, Bendigo, and Rushworth might sometimes be found to be still worth while trying for alluvial deposits. The mere fact that gold was found in liberal quantities on many of these fields would point to the possibility of many minor leads or deposits having been over-looked.

It is a recognised fact that wherever alluvial gold has been discovered on Victorian goldfields, there is existent somewhere nearby the quartz reefs from which the alluvial supply came. In many cases, whilst free gold has been discovered in many localities, subsequent search has failed to identify the quartz reefs or veins. Commonsense, together with geological formulas, would point to these reefs being in existence, consequently they are yet awaiting discovery.

It behoves the prospector, therefore, once he has located a certain line, to work ever upward so as to discover the parent reef or indicator. It is now that a hammer or a drill or the magnifying glass will be of particular value. Once this reef or indicator has been located, it is advisable to take prospects from different points of the reef.

The quartz and rubble and any fragments of earthy substance adhering to this reef must be broken and samples from various sections of it broken up and washed. The panning-off will soon show whether there is any sign of color in the prospect. Should this dish washing prove encouraging and give average results of color for a number of washings, it might be well to arrange for a crushing of, say, a couple of tons of the ore.

Should the results of this crushing prove favourable, it may well happen that a new goldfield might be opened up or a long dormant one revived and given a new lease of life.

CHAPTER 3.

TOOLS OF THE TRADE.

The amateur prospector does not need to over-burden himself with a too formidable array of tools. Indeed, the business of fossicking for gold can be carried on with a minimum of appliances. The more commonly used tools are a miner's pick, two shovels (one long and the other short handled), and a panning dish. When sinking holes the single-headed pick will be found to be the more service-able, whilst for other and more open work the double-headed variety is the more practicable.

With these few tools of trade the amateur can fossick about and quite conceivably achieve some good results.

Later as he gains in experience or should he decide to strike out and prospect new ground, he will find it neces-sary to add somewhat to this list of tools. A magnifying glass, a file, an assortment of drills, a hammer and some quick-silver are other accessories, all of which will be found to be of use at various times.

The following are the more intricate of the methods and machinery used for the obtaining of the precious mineral.

The Panning Dish.

The use of the panning dish is the simplest and most elementary method employed by the prospector to separate possible traces of gold from its generally associated sub-stances, such as clay, gravel, earth, etc. The dish or pan used is a shallow sheet iron (not galvanised iron nor tin) dish, which can be purchased at any hardware store for the sum of two or three shillings. There are several sizes available, the most generally used being about ten inches in diameter at the bottom and about 16 inches diameter at the top. The prospector takes a partly filled dish of wash-dirt, together with a quantity of water. If it is possible to place the dish half submerged in running water, so much the better.

He then proceeds to puddle, or "mud-pie" the mixture with his hands; gradually all the clayey material and all the larger stones or pebbles are removed from the dish. The dish is rotated gently, whilst by degrees the stuff is care-fully examined and smaller stones removed by hand, until there is eventually left in the dish only the very fine stuff.

When at last there remain in the dish only a small quantity of water and sand, an occasional twirl around will enable the prospector to ascertain if there exists any sign of "color."

If any show appears the remaining sand is gradually washed clear from the gold. There is a certain art in the handling of even this simple appliance, but constant practice will quickly bring to one the best and most efficient style of using it.

One cubic yard of material in place is equal to about 200 dishes of loose gravel, so payable ground will need to

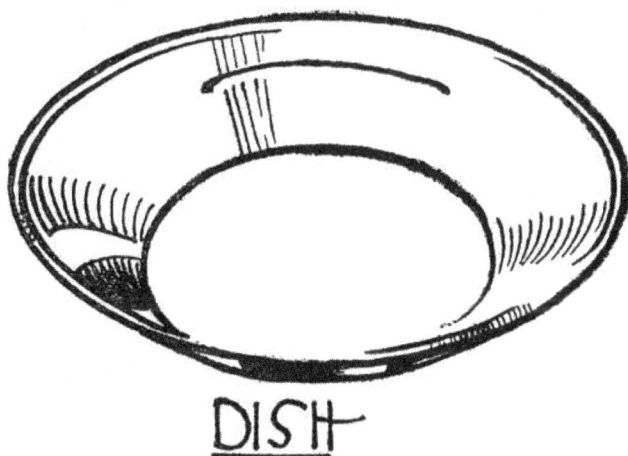

DISH

show only a small tail of gold in the dish, i.e., a thirtieth $(\frac{1}{30})$ of a grain of gold, actually only a few flyspecks, at 2d. per grain would mean over one shilling per cubic yard as the value of the ground.

The Puddling Tub.

This consists simply of one-half of a small cask or barrel placed on a foundation of rocks or planks of timber. Very much the same principle as that on which the panning dish is worked is here employed.

A quantity of wash-dirt is placed in the tub, together with a quantity of water. A broad wooden spade serves to puddle the mixture. The process of tilting the tub and thus pouring off the water thick with clay is carried on, new

water being constantly added, until at length the clear
water and the washed gravel and sand remain in the tub.

By tilting and lowering alternately the sides of the
tub, the stuff can be washed to one side, whereupon if gold
is present, it will be found to lie along the edge of the stuff
at the bottom of the tub. The construction of this puddling
tub is often dependant upon circumstances. In place of a
half-barrel, a section of a hollow tree might be adopted to
the purpose. In this instance, some method of running off
the sludge can be devised.

The Cradle.

As the name implies, this is usually an oblong box,
with one end open and so arranged on rockers that it can
be rocked from side to side in a similar manner to an infant's
cradle.

The top portion of the cradle consists of a sieve with
a large number of holes, none of which should exceed half
an inch in length. The more and smaller the holes are the
better will be the results in handling. Below this are placed
two slides, one of which protrudes from the rear end of the
cradle and slopes downwards towards the front. The other
slide projects from the front of the cradle and slopes towards the rear of the box, immediately below the first slide.

On both of these slides are fitted several riffles, that
is, short strips of wood, which will form crevices to hold
any gold which might be contained in the stuff being washed
through the cradle. The floor of the cradle is built on a
slope also, with a number of riffles placed so as to again
intercept any stray particles of gold that may have passed
the riffles on the slides.

The operation consists of placing on the sieve a quantity of the stuff which has already been puddled and freed
from clay. The cradle is rocked to and fro as water is
poured on to the stuff being treated. The water and fine
stuff is carried through the sieve on to each slide in turn,
and eventually, runs off the floor board. Any gold present
will be held by the riffles. After several washings the slides
may be lifted and any gold caught by them recovered.

Should it be possible to cover the slides and floor of
the cradle with bagging or canvas, this is recommended as
this covering will be found to hold the gold more securely
than the flat wooden surface.

The Puddling Machine.

This is simply a trough built in circular formation on slightly raised ground. The inner and outer sides of this trough are carefully lined with pieces of timber.

A long arm of timber works on a pivot in the centre. The longer end of this arm projects beyond the trough, and at the end a horse it harnessed. To either end of the arm are attached harrows, one close to the horse and one at the other end.

As the horse moves around, the harrows are set in motion around the trough. The stuff being treated is thrown into the trough, together with a quantity of water. The action of the harrows moving around the trough puddles the mixture, and the sludge formed is drained off. This process is carried on until the mixture is clean enough to allow the gold to be separated.

The puddling machine is generally used in situations when water is not handy close by the scene of operations, and, consequently, has to be conveyed over some distance.

A reconstructed puddling machine at Wrooh, Victoria
(courtesy the Victorian Hertage Database).

CHAPTER 4.

TOOLS OF THE TRADE—Continued.

Sluices.

In places where there is an abundance of water and it is considered worth while to treat large quantities of wash dirt, it will be found advisable to erect sluices. These consist of long wooden troughs about 12 inches deep, and from 18 to 24 inches in width. The length of each is about 10 to 12 feet, and the ends are made to slightly taper off, so that they can be made to fit into one another and so increase the length of the sluice.

The longer these sluices are the better will be their efficiency as the greater length enables the pay dirt to be broken up more thoroughly, and also a larger number of riffle-bars to be used. Two hundred feet of sluice is not too great a length when a number of men are shovelling. By this manner many tons of stuff may be treated in a day.

Under the Mining By-laws one sluice head equals one cubic foot of water per second or 3600 cubic feet per hour. The cubic feet of gravel this quantity will sluice depends upon the grade of sluice box. On a grade of 6 inches in 12 feet or 1 in 24 a sluice head will treat 3600 divided by 24; or 150 cubic feet (5½ cubic yards) of average gravel per hour, and so for steeper or flatter working grades.

Several of these boxes are placed in line to constitute a long wooden trough, which is so arranged that there is a gradual fall throughout the entire length. The head of the trough or sluice is so arranged that it receives a flow of water from some ledge or cutaway in the bank of a stream of running water. At various parts of the boxes riffle bars are placed so as to catch the gold. When placing the riffle bars in the boxes, it is advisable to fix these into their position by wedging rather than by nailing. They can then be removed from time to time whilst the process of cleaning up and recovering the gold is in progress.

Double Sluices.

These are sometimes used where there is a particularly good force of water available, or where two parties of men are working in close conjunction. Wider boxes are constructed with boards placed down the centre. The use of double sluices enable the process of washing to be carried on continuously, as when one side is held up for cleaning, washing may be proceeded with in the other and vice versa.

It is not essential, of course, that the bottoms of these sluices be made of wood. Rocks, fairly smooth for preference, or pitchers or cobblestones serve equally well, and oftentimes are more effective in retaining the gold.

Ground Sluicing.

A ground sluice is a ditch cut into the surface rock formation and designed on a similar manner to the wooden sluice. This form of sluice is particularly applicable to a situation where there is a good flow of water and a certain fall in elevation to enable the sluice to be cut in such a manner that a stream of running water can easily be diverted into it.

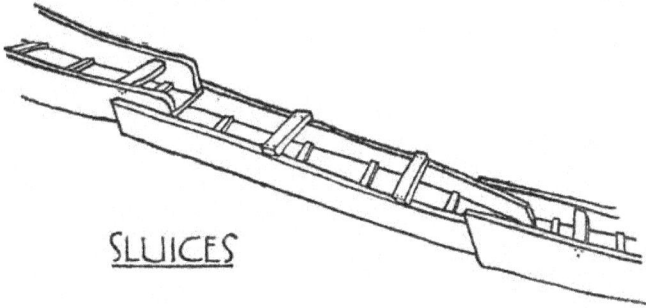

SLUICES

The sides of the sluice may be lined with timber or large stones, whilst riffles are provided by ledges of rock or wooden fixtures. It will be necessary to arrange what is known as a tail race or canal to enable the water and dirt after treatment to escape far enough to prevent its obstructing operations.

The Whip.

The whip is a method used for the easier removal of the overburden when shafting or driving is being maintained to a deep level.

The innovation consists simply of a strong beam of timber implanted in the ground at an angle so that the end overhangs the position of the shaft being sunk. A simple method of pulley and tackle is arranged, and by means of horsepower this is a practical and simple method of removing ore to the surface.

The Dolly.

Small quantities of quartz can be treated by means of a mortar and pestle. This method is known as hand

dollying.   An iron hammer or wooden instrument with an
iron-shod head will serve to pound the quartz, which is
then placed in a pan and carefully washed for color.

The Windlass.

The windlass is a well-known contrivance, which is
often made use of for raising quantities of ore from shafts
or for lowering miners to work at various levels.

In addition to the above, there have been many other
devices tried out at various diggings with more or less success.   In some cases, extensive use has been made of hydraulic sluicing, which method will be dealt with more fully
later. Of the others, the Californian Pump, a system of feed
belt running over rollers and having buckets attached at
various intervals, and the Whim, a method involving a
spindle and drum and used for the treating of large quantities of ore are the better known.

It has invariably been proved that for the purpose of
winning gold, men have used, firstly, whatever appliances
most suited the peculiar circumstances under which gold
was discovered by them. As a rule, at first, the pick, shovel
and pan were utilized, later came the hand dolly and the
puddling machine. Then as the gold gave further promise
the windlass and bucket, and the sluice were called into
action, being at length replaced in some of the large mines
by electrically driven apparatus.

The last working windlass in Victoria, at Clunes 1971.

CHAPTER 5.

HYDRAULIC MINING.

It will be readily perceived that the proximity of water and its possibilities of use are important factors in gold prospecting, which must not be under estimated. The prospector or fossicker, if he can work close to a running creek, will soon find that it is a very great advantage to be able to apply water-power to his operations.

Later as time goes on and he finds it necessary to treat still larger quantities of pay-dirt, he will again have recourse to the use of water by means of sluices, long-toms or hydraulic sluices.

PUDDLING MACHINE.

The long-tom was at one time used very extensively in Victoria, having been introduced by Californian miners, who came to the colony during the early gold rush periods. It has practically ceased being in use, but a short description might not be amiss:—

It was composed of two long boxes similar somewhat to ordinary wooden sluices, except that the width was about twice as great. One box was placed under the other. The upper box was free from riffles, whilst at the lower end a grating was placed so that the water and finer stuff could fall into the box beneath. All large stones stayed on top of the grating and were removed by hand.

In the lower box were placed riffles so that the gold might be caught here and the lighter stuff be carried away on the flow of water. The higher box was generally built narrower at one end, where a stream of water was diverted or directed into it, and wider at the other end so that the stuff being treated might be the more easily handled.

The long-tom required only a moderate flow of water, and its use enabled a considerable amount of stuff to be treated in a comparatively short time. Eventually, however, it fell into disuse and was more or less replaced by hydraulic sluicing.

Hydraulic sluicing was often resorted to in the early days, in situations where a good pressure of water was available at a higher level than the ground being worked. A pipe line was laid to the nearest flow of water, and the pressure of water enabled great masses of earth to be broken up and treated. Where a number of men are working and a fair quantity of wash-dirt is to be treated, a system of hydraulic washing can be organised. The amateur prospector of the present day will, however, probably not interest himself in such bulk handling of wash-dirt. When he has discovered a deposit of pay-dirt of sufficient quantity to be worked in this manner, he will in all likelihood open negotiations with a mining company to do this work.

Sluicing in a creek in Victoria, 1935.

CHAPTER 6.

HOW GOLD IS FORMED.

Gold is a metallic chemical substance, and is probably the most sought after mineral in the world. It is found in many countries, but Australia has been one of the most prolific producers. Much gold has already been won here, and it is certain that much more still remains to be discovered.

That gold strikes of equal importance to, and of possibly even greater value than those already exploited may yet be discovered, and will sooner or later astound the world, is the hope of many mining and geological experts.

The mineral is found either in its native state as "free gold" or, more frequently, in conjunction with other minerals such as lead, silver or tellurium. Very fine quantities are often found associated with iron, pyrites and other minerals. Gold is found in quartz veins, and in the debris deposited by recent and ancient streams in the gullies and basins which formed their beds. Sometimes it appears in the form of crystals—sometimes as nuggets, and at other times as thin as the finest gold leaf.

A general study of the rocks and their formations, which are most likely to yield gold cannot fail to be of interest to the man who is going out for gold. Geologists tell us that gold was formed very early in the earth's history, and that consequently it is only in the older rock formations that gold originated.

It has oftentimes been discovered in situations where the newer or more modern formations predominate. This apparent phenomenon is explained by the probability that the deposits located have broken away from the original reef or vein through disintegration and denudation of the parent lode by storms, weather conditions, subterranean disturbances or other abnormal occurrences.

Of the primary or oldest rocks, the most likely to contain auriferous strata are the upper and lower order of silurian rocks. These include sandstones, slates, clays and conglomerates. A visit to the Geological Museum in Spring Street will impress the nature of these formations upon the memory far more easily than ever so much reading about them would do.

Gold may be discovered in granite or diorite, in the silurian sandstones and slates, and the tertiary deposits.

Usually it is discovered in the form of fine particles, but occasionally in lumps or nuggets or in fine minute wafer-like fragments. Gold deposits may be classed under two distinct headings—veins or reefs and placer or alluvial. Much of the later gold produced at the large goldfields, such as Ballarat or Bendigo has been recovered by quartz mining from the reefs and veins.

In alluvial deposits gold is usually found in the gravel, earthy or clayey matter, which has been washed by rain or stream into the low lying portions of basins, creek beds, etc. As a general rule the ore from reef mining is treated by means of crushing and amalgamation, whilst in alluvial working the process of washing by pan or cradle or sluicing is the more generally used.

The Deep Leads of Victoria.

It has been ascertained that many of the gold deposits of Victoria lie in a series of deep leads extending more or less diagonally across the state.

Interpretation clause number 2 of the 14th section of the Mining Development Act, passed in 1896, gives the definition of a deep lead as "any watercourse or gutter below the surface of the earth containing alluvial deposits at a depth of not less than one hundred feet from such surface."

These deep leads are in reality the present day forms of rivers which thousands of years ago ran either north or south across the country. These rivers had their sources in a watershed, which in all probability coincided to some measure with what we at the present day know as the great Divide of Victoria.

That these ancient rivers were very similar in appearance and characteristics to our present day rivers has been ascertained by reason of the presence in the gravels of leaves, tree-trunks and other fossil remains embedded in the stratum and rock formations.

It is assumed then that in that remote period the auriferous washings from the hillsides and outcropping strata had by means of floods and other weather elements been deposited in the beds, bends and between boulders in the creek and river beds.

As time went on new formations of rock and earth covered these deposits, and new rivers and creeks flowed across the country at higher levels. In some cases the original auriferous strata lay sufficiently high to escape being entirely submerged, whilst in other instances they, together with the washings and debris from them, were buried at much greater depths.

As a general rule it has been found that in Victoria those leads trending southwards lie at a higher altitude than those directed north. This may be accounted for by the possibility of some greater subsidence in the north or a gradual subterranean uplift in the southern parts.

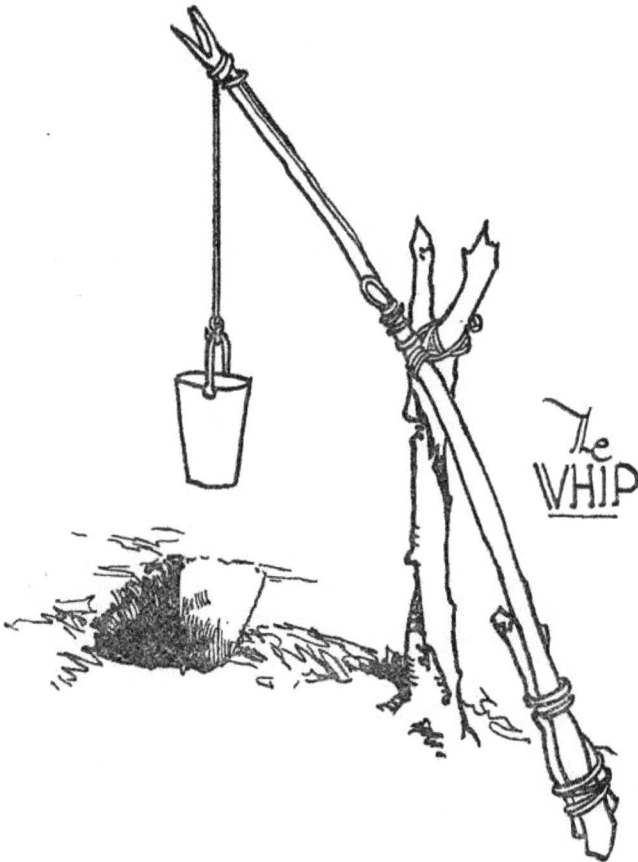

The WHIP

CHAPTER 7.

SOME NOTES ON VICTORIAN GOLDFIELDS.

No work of fiction ever written can compare with the romance and splendid history of the discovery and development of the goldfields of Victoria.

For close on 50 years after the discovery in 1802 of Port Phillip, the country lying in the South-eastern portion of the continent was valued only in the terms of cattle grazing. The value of the large tracts of land settled upon was computed according to the number of cattle it was possible to graze thereon.

The discovery of a small quantity of gold in the Pyrenees was the cause of directing the attention of the citizens of Melbourne towards the possibilities of gold being found in payable quantities, and thus assisting the laudable object of attracting additional population to the colony of Port Phillip.

Consequent on the reward of 200 guineas being offered for the discovery of a goldfield within 200 miles of Melbourne, small parcels of gold began to arrive in Melbourne from various isolated sources.

Then in 1851, only a few months after the reward had been offered, came astounding news from several districts where men had been quietly working. Started then the mad stampede to Ballarat, Bendigo, Mount Alexander and other parts when gold-finds had been reported.

In the "Argus," of October 4th, 1851, we read:—"It is the intention of two captains at present here to proceed to the diggings at once and satisfy themselves of the truth of the astounding intelligence that continues to pour in; and if there is no exaggeration they intend immediately on their return to moor their vessels snugly and start with their crews to the diggings."

In a matter of about two months 67,000 ozs. of gold were obtained, whilst the yield of gold for the following year was estimated at 2,286,535 ozs. The number of miners on the two largest fields, Ballarat and Bendigo, was between 70,000 and 80,000.

The discovery of gold in many parts of the State was the direct cause of hundreds of towns springing up. Many of these habitations are now but ghosts, overgrown and deserted whilst others, though in most cases not commanding the same numbers in population, have thrived and become permanent.

Before setting out on his quest the intending prospector will probably welcome some few notes on the more likely fields for operations, and the following few remarks may assist him in this direction. The fact that localities·other than mentioned have been ignored does not, of course, preclude the possibilities of these sections carrying gold.

But the average beginner, setting out, will most probably prefer to go at once to country which is known to have some definite prospects of early results.

The Eastern Goldfields.

Starting out from Melbourne and lying close to the metropolis, we have a group of fields comprising those of Eltham, Warrandyte, Warburton, Emerald, Gembrook, and the various tributaries of the Yarra. From the Yarra to the Goulburn are numerous scattered workings, including Queenstown, Yea River and Reedy Creek, now better known as Tyaak.

Localities worked all through this area have richly rewarded those who have worked them, and for many years now desultory prospecting and fossicking have been done generally by old-timers, into whose blood the gold fever has penetrated never to be again lost.

Eastwards from Port Phillip Bay and running due north to the Goulburn River is a huge belt of silurian country. In this tract of country lie many auriferous localities, which cannot be said to conform to any clearly defined system of reef-belts.

All sections of this country has yielded results to both quartz and alluvial workings, although to date only work of a very superficial nature has been carried on.

This field of action is close to the metropolis, and conditions of working are pleasant—plenty of wood and water are available, and no serious obstacles are offered to the gold seeker.

Further to the east lie two great belts of proved auriferous country. The first of these belts takes as its pivot the country around Alexandra, and runs north to Merton and south to the ranges south of Darlingford. The second belt of gold country comprises the well-known fields of Walhalla, Matlock, Gaffney's Creek, Jamieson and other fields, some of which are still being worked. Here was a scene of great activity in the early days. Dozens of diggings were scattered among the hills and creeks from Mansfield to Woods Point and Walhalla and among the tributaries of the Upper Yarra.

Famous old names of diggings in these parts are Jericho on the Jordan, Red Jacket and Blue Jacket. The diggings of Red Jacket were named by the passengers on board the sailing ship "Red Jacket," practically all of whom, when landed in Melbourne, made straight for the diggings.

PUDDLING TUB

Discoveries of gold are still being made in these parts, and these tend to foreshadow a fair prospect of success for any organised search.

East from Walhalla lies Donnelly's Creek, where many rich reefs were at one time worked. Much detailed work has been carried out in this section from time to time, but no appreciable success in locating the old quartz reefs has been experienced.

East again from this point, little gold has been discovered until we come to the Mitchell and King Rivers, the first of which flows south towards the Gippsland Lakes and the other running north to join the Ovens at Wangaratta.

From these rivers to the extreme boundaries of the State lie great stretches of more or less possible gold-bear-ing country. Many of the belts in these districts yielded very rich results, and in some cases are still being worked. Rutherglen, Chiltern, Omeo, The Dargo and Beechworth are fields rich in possibilities.

In the early days, thousands of Chinese miners worked the alluvial river and creek beds at Merrijig and other famous diggings in these mountainous districts.

Northwards the Kiewa River valley holds much auriferous country, from which much gold was taken in the early days. Difficulties experienced in working the wet ground encountered in this valley dissuaded many attempts to work these diggings thoroughly.

It has been estimated that in this district are some five hundred square miles of auriferous country, the greater part of which consists of terraces, spurs and gullies. The alluvial diggings at Stanley, Clear Lake and Yackandandah, Rowdy Flats and Osborne Flats were particularly noted for their richness in gold.

East of the Kiewa Valley, the Mitta Mitta River drains some 2,000 square miles of more or less auriferous country. Much gold has been recovered from the numerous small tributaries of the Mitta Mitta. Many alluvial reefs discovered in these parts have not been fully exploited.

The Ovens Valley consists of a large area drained by the Ovens River and its tributaries, principal of which are the Buffalo River, Buckland River, Hodgson's Creek and the King River. These streams drain a large area, with definite auriferous showings. Rich alluvial deposits have been worked throughout the hills extending from the main Divide to Rutherglen.

A feature of the gold found in this district was its extreme fineness, and this would seem to point to the theory that rich auriferous reefs must exist somewhere about the head-waters of these streams.

Clunes.

To Clunes is due the honour of being the first goldfield in Victoria. The quartz reefs of Clunes were being heavily worked until late in the 'nineties. The lodes at Clunes were located in slate and sandstone beds, and the quartz was mined to the considerable depths of 1,100 and 1,745 feet.

The alluvial deposits of Clunes, and also of Creswick and Carisbrook, form part of the Berry-Moolort-Loddon deep lead system, the northern extremity of which is in the vicinity of Inglewood and Kingower.

This deep lead proved to be one of the best gold-producing leads in Victoria.

In addition to quartz mining, much alluvial work was done at Clunes, which produced gold in excellent quantities.

Creswick.

The Creswick and adjoining goldfields are situated on a number of out-thrusts from the Ordovician deep lead, which runs under the plains of basalt adjacent to Creswick.

Much gold was obtained at Creswick in shallow alluvial gutters. This is a district in which the reopening of some of the old alluvial washes might well prove profitable.

Ballarat.

This well-known goldfield does not need any introduction. All over the world the Ballarat goldfields are famous. In the early days, thousands of diggers from California and other parts of the world arrived in Melbourne en route for Ballarat. Gold was easily got at Ballarat, it was got in good payable quantities, and at one time it held a population of some fifty or sixty thousand.

The gold at Ballarat has invariably been found in Ordovician slates and sandstones. In parts of this field extensive reefs are frequent, and beds of quartz sometimes 350 feet in width have produced enormous quantities of payable ore.

Typical indicators at Ballarat consist of thin pyritic seams and beds of slate.

Much gold has been found at Ballarat, and at no time since its discovery has mining for gold on its fields entirely ceased. A nugget, named the "Welcome Nugget" was found at Ballarat in 1858, and weighed 2,217 ozs. of gross weight, and was found 180 feet from the surface.

Bendigo.

At Bendigo are found the deepest mines in Australia. The extent of auriferous workings at Bendigo cover an area of some 15 miles by 3 miles. Gold has been won in Bendigo to depths of over 4,000 feet, the deepest shaft being 4,616 feet.

In recent years Bendigo has been considered the chief mining district of the State. The production of gold from Bendigo mines during 1913 was 168,172 ozs., and although much of the gold has been located at considerable depths, it is quite possible that higher reefs may yet be found here. The total output from Bendigo mines up to the end of 1930 approximated 20,619,086 ozs., or 631 tons, valued in the region of £83,000,000.

Dunolly.

Lying due north of Ballarat and west of Bendigo are many goldfields of proven worth. A feature of the early mining at Dunolly was the large number of fair-sized nuggets found there. The neighbouring country around Dunolly was at one time referred to as "being rotten with gold."

Very heavy gold was a feature of the Dunolly diggings, and much gold in nuggets was obtained from outcropping reefs. It was at Moliagul, a few miles north of Dunolly, that, on the 5th of February, 1869, the "Welcome Stranger," possibly the most famous of all Australian nuggets was discovered by John Deason and Richard Oates.

This mass of gold was discovered practically on the surface, and within two feet of the sandstone bedrock, resting on a bank of stiff clay. Whilst mixed with some quartz, the major portion of the nugget was solid gold.

VINDLASS

A report on this nugget made at the time says:—"The gold of this nugget, from the crucible assays, I found to be 98.66 per cent. of pure gold. It thus contains only 1.75 per cent. of alloy, composed chiefly of silver and iron. The melted gold, with that given to their friends by the fortunate finders, amounted to 2,280 ozs., or 2,248 ozs. of pure gold, its value at the Bank of England being £9,534.

Castlemaine.

The Castlemaine diggings were originally known as the Mount Alexander Goldfields, and a wealth of gold was taken from the shallow alluvial workings. On this field the gold appeared generally in spurs or isolated patches, due, it is thought, to the presence of many faults and folds in the strata.

Early in the history of the Mount Alexander diggings the miners flocked to it in thousands from Ballarat and Bendigo, having been drawn to it by reason of glowing reports concerning its wealth of gold and the easy accessibility of the rich auriferous workings. The shallow alluvial ground was then worked very thoroughly.

Daylesford.

The gold at Daylesford was generally found in fault lodes, showing through the Ordovician sandstones. Some of the gold on this field was discovered at around 500 feet of sinking. Many mines were worked at Daylesford, some of the lodes being very prolific.

Other rich fields were developed at Lauriston, Stawell, St. Arnaud, and at Bethanga, on the Upper Murray. Space does not permit an exhaustive list of the many smaller and lesser-known fields, but it is certain that over the greater part of Victoria exist vast possibilities for the discovery of gold.

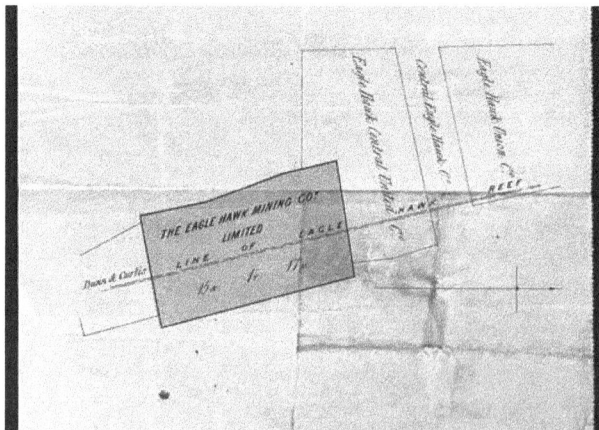

GEOLOGICAL MAP OF

VICTORIA

SCALE OF MILES

0   25   50   75   100

CAINOZOIC.
Soil, Clays, Sandstones, Brown Coal and Limestone.

JURASSIC.
Felspathic Sandstones and Mudstones with Black Coal.

PERMO-CARBONIFEROUS AND CARBONIFEROUS.
Sandstones and Glacial Deposits.

DEVONIAN.
Sandstones, Limestones, Shales and Volcanic Rocks.

SILURIAN.
Sandstones, Mudstones, Slates, and Limestones.

ORDOVICIAN.
Slates and Sandstones.

HEATHCOTIAN.
Cherts, Diabase, and Tuffs.

METAMORPHIC.
In part Pre-Ordovician.

CAINOZOIC BASALT.

DACITE AND PORPHYRIES.

GRANITIC ROCKS.

Map of Victoria from *Prospector's Guide : Victoria* (1932).
Map over the following three pages is from *Getting Gold* (1931).

SOUTH AUSTRALIA

KARKAROOC

WEEAH

Sand Hills & Heath

Manangarang

Kulwin

Piangil

Murrayville   Underbool

Cowangie

Pinnaroo

Tiega   Ouyen

Waipanp

Tooleybuc

Nyah

Chittingollah

Castle Donnington

L. Tyrrell

Sea Lake

Boigbeat

Berriwillock

Woomelang

Kamcira

TATCHERA

Lake Charm

Kerang

Lascootta

Yaapeet   Turpatown

Rainbow

Beulah

Coyura

Rosebery

Hopetown

Birchip

L. HINDMARSH   Willenabrina

Yanac   Lorquon   Nurrip

Brim   Warren

Watchem

Wycheproof

Bungaluke   Roop

Narmal

Wychitella

Buckrabanyule

Mitre

Antwerp

Warracknabeal

Morton

Minyip

Watcher   Morey

Woorooganook

M't Jeffcott   Charlton

M't Korong

Inglewood

Kellalac   Booloom

Tarranginnie   Brung

Donald

Coonooer

Wedderburn

Kingspoint

Kerang

Lillimur N.   Diapur

Kaniva   Miram   Nhill

Lawloit   Kiata

Dimboola   Marra Marra   Minyip

Burrereo

Kewell   Pimpinio

KARA KARA

Cope Cope

GLADSTONE

WEEAH   LOWAN

Sandy Desert with Mallee

Martat   Natimuk

Mooreapkl   Gymbowen

Bachinis

Naradjuha

Apsley

Toolonno

B. Edenhope

Harrow

GLENELG

Wotjye

Balmoral

Chetwynd   Cavendish

Dergholm   Narrea

Horsham

BARUNG

Clenorchy

Stawell

Mt Wm

Gt William

Crowlands

Banyena   Langsrren

Kalkee

Marroona

RIPON

Ararat

Buangor   Trawalla

Beaufort

KARA KARA   Marnoo

St Arnaud

Cro Cro

Stuart Hill   Archdale

Dunolly

Natteyyook

Maldon

Rheola   Tarnagulla

Moliagul

BALLARAT

DUNDAS

Carapook

Castlerton   Sandford

Coleraine

M't Clinton Hill

Hopperkir

Dunkeld

Glenthompson

Pickliffe

Streatham

FOLLETT

Merino

Digby

Casterton

Bradholme

Branxholme

Byaduk

Purdeal

Hamilton

Penshurst

Caramut

Derrinallum

Darlington

Wiarlake

GRENVILLE

HAMPDEN

NORMANBY

Macarthur

Heywood

VILLIERS

Ensdale

Illowa

Woolsthorpe

Ballangeich

Mortlake

Noorat

Terang

Cressy

DISCOVERY BAY

Portland

PORTLAND B.

Narrawong

Fairy

Warrnambool

Allansford

Framlingham

HEYTESBURY

Timboon

Port Campbell

Colac

POLWARTH

C. Bridgewater

CAPE OTWAY

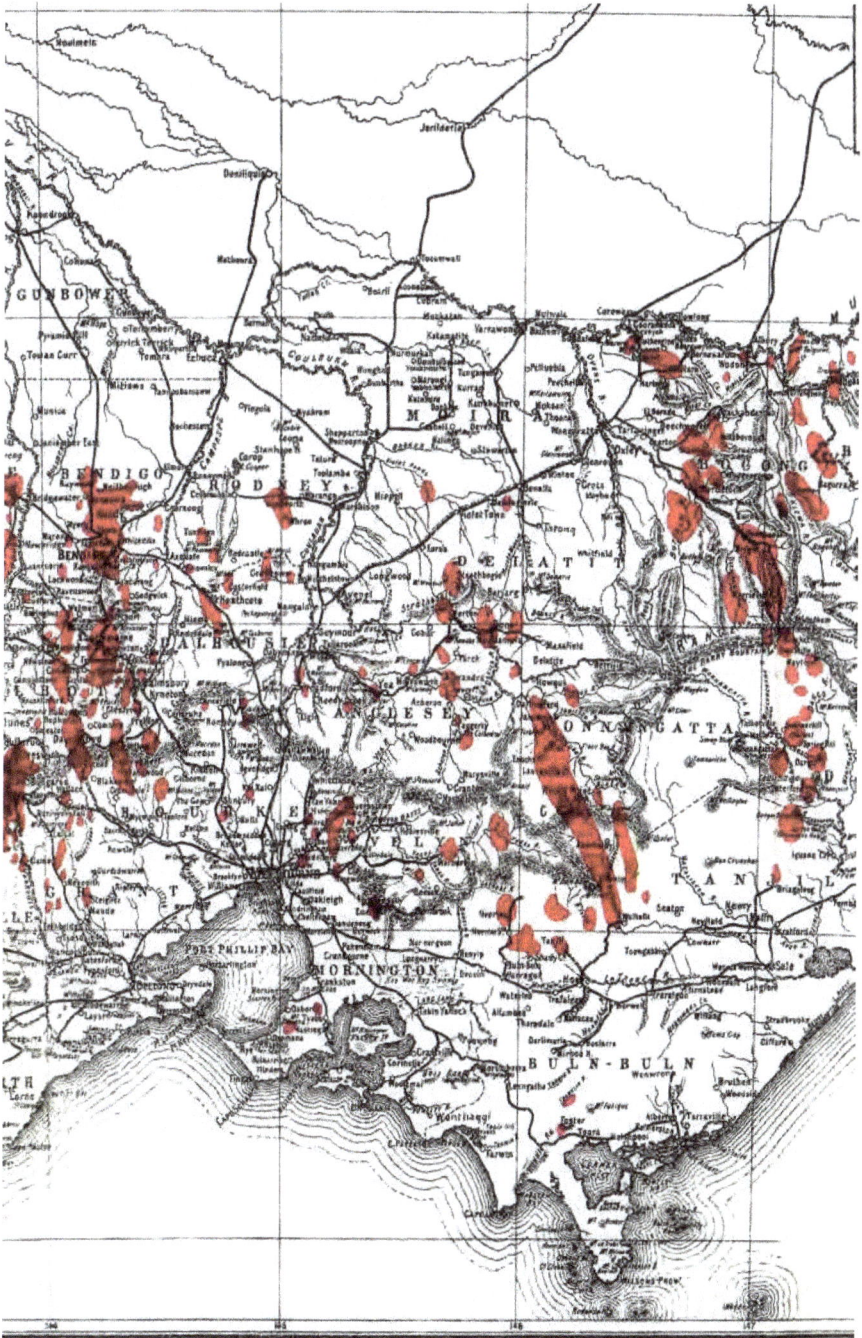

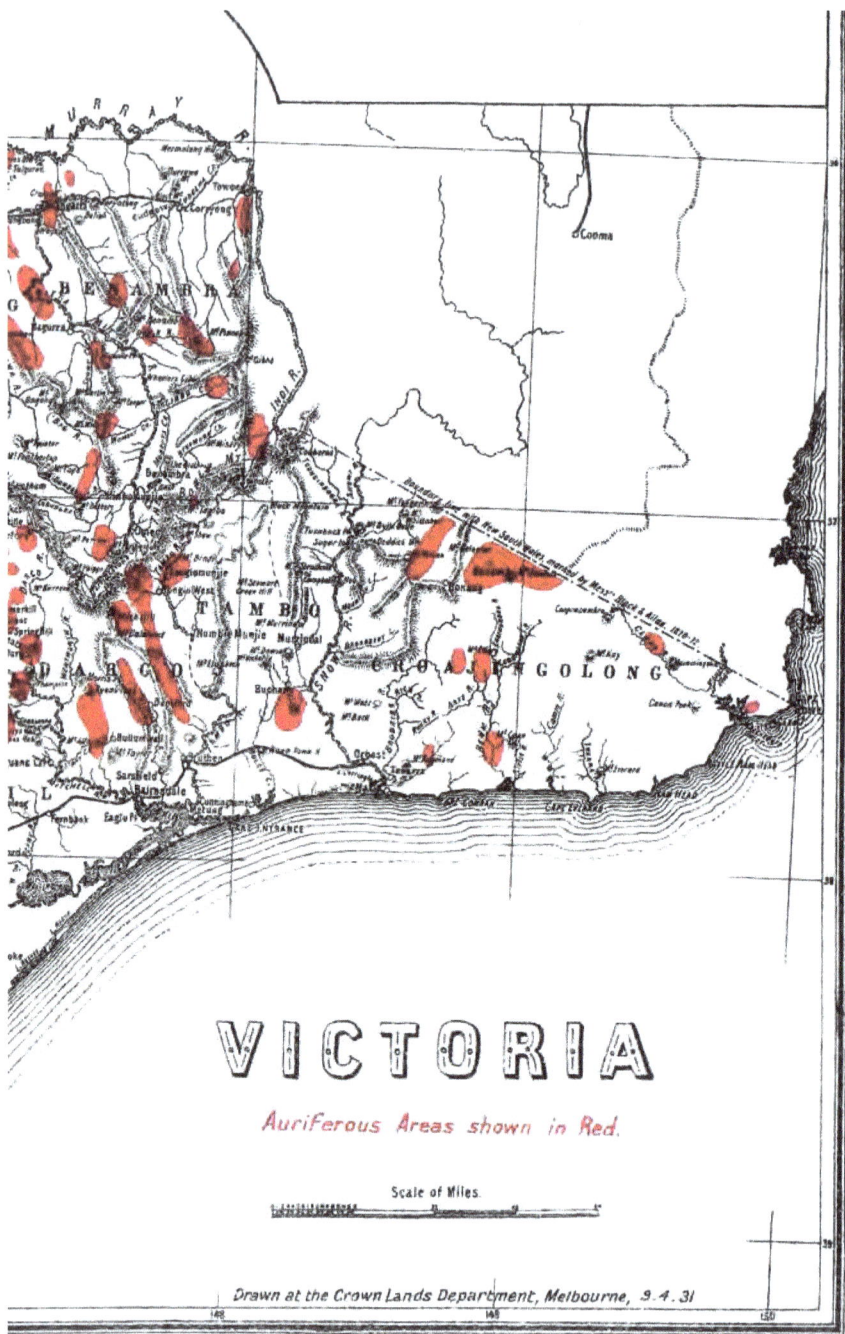

VICTORIA

Auriferous Areas shown in Red.

Scale of Miles.

Drawn at the Crown Lands Department, Melbourne, 9.4.31

CHAPTER VIII.

STATE BATTERIES.

It is possible that the prospector may wish to be aware of the localities where State Batteries are situated. With this knowledge in hand, he may then choose his scene of operations at some situation in handy reach of a battery.

The fees charged are:—6/- per ton, minimum charge of 30/- (five tons). Where yield of gold is less than 6 dwts. per ton, and quartz carted over three miles, a rebate of 6d. per mile per ton is allowed. Minimum fee in this case, £1.

The following is a list of State Batteries and their locations:—

A LIST OF STATE BATTERIES.

No.	Battery.	Foreman's Headquarters Situated at
1	Ararat	Maryborough
2	Ballarat East	Creswick
3	Chewton	Creswick
4	Chiltern	Eaglehawk
5	Creswick	Creswick
6	Daylesford	Creswick
7	Dunolly	Maryborough
8	Egerton	Creswick
9	Glen Wills	Sunnyside
10	Grant	Inspector of Mines, Melbourne
11	Granya	Eaglehawk
12	Inglewood	Maryborough or Eaglehawk
13	Italian Gully	Creswick
14	Koetong	Eaglehawk
15	Landsborough	Maryborough
16	Lauriston	Creswick
17	Maldon	Maldon
18	Maryborough	Maryborough
19	Omeo	Omeo
20	Queenstown	Creswick
21	Rutherglen	Eaglehawk
22	Stawell	Maryborough
23	Sunnyside	Sunnyside
24	Tarnagulla	Maryborough

25	. . ..	Moliagul	Maryborough or Eaglehawk
26	. . ..	Walhalla	Walhalla
27	. . ..	Wedderburn	Maryborough
28	. . ..	Wingan	Inspector of Mines, Melbourne
29	. . ...	Reedy Creek	Inspector of Mines, Melbourne

CHAPTER IX.

MINERS' RIGHTS.

Miner's Right.—A person making application **for** the registration of a claim, or other privilege, under these By-laws, shall, at the time of making such application, produce to the Registrar the miner's right or miners' rights under which such application is made.

The intending prospector will probably find of value some information concerning Miners' Rights, what they mean, what privileges they confer, their cost, and where they may be obtained.

Any person may obtain a miner's right upon payment of two shillings and sixpence at the Receipt and Pay Office, Melbourne, or from country clerks of courts, or from most of the mining registrars, and such right shall remain in force for one year.

Privileges Conferred on Holders of Miner's Rights.

(Section 5, *Mines Act* 1928.)

The holder of a miner's right is entitled to take possession for gold-mining purposes of such areas of Crown Land as the by-laws shall permit. He is also entitled, subject to such by-laws, to cut, construct, and use races, dams and reservoirs for mining through and upon Crown lands, and to use such water for mining for gold and for his domestic purposes; also subject to the Forests Act to cut any live or dead timber, except blackwood, and to remove the same, and to strip and remove the bark from any such timber, and also to remove any stone or gravel for mining purposes, or for fuel or otherwise for his personal use, from any Crown lands not excepted or exempted from occupation for mining, and also to make tramways or other roads for the carrying out of his operations.

CHAPTER X.

SOME EXTRACTS FROM THE MINING BY-LAWS.

Some reference to the mining by-laws of the State will in all probability be found necessary, and to this purpose some extracts from the by-laws are appended herewith. These give general information and advice to the prospector concerning the problems he is most likely to need advice on, but for more fully-detailed information the enquirer is urged to obtain a copy of the complete Mining By-laws, which may be obtained on application to the Mines Department.

The following extracts are taken from the Mining By-laws of the State of Victoria, as published in the *Government Gazette* of 19th February, 1931, pp. 617-640:—

CROWN LAND.

"Crown Land" includes all lands of the Crown, also all lands entered upon, marked out, or taken possession of, held, occupied, worked, or used under and by virtue of a miner's right and the provisions of Part 2 of the *Mines Act*, 1928 (Part 2 relates to private land).

MINING BY-LAWS—EXTRACTS.

By-law No. 3.—Claims.—General Rules.

Unless otherwise prescribed, a claim shall be taken possession of by erecting at each angle of its boundaries a post at least 3 inches in diameter and not less than 3 feet above the ground. A V-trench shall be cut 6 inches in depth, and shall extend at least 3 feet from each post along each boundary line of the claim.

Where it is not practicable to comply with the above provisions, it shall be sufficient to drive an iron peg firmly in the ground at each angle of the claim.

A claim shall be registered as prescribed herein.

A claim shall be worked in accordance with these By-laws.

1. *Mode of Registration.*—An ordinary quartz claim, a quartz prospecting claim, a quartz prospecting area, a quartz tunnelling claim, an alluvial claim, a mineral claim, and a mineral prospecting claim, shall be registered in the manner following:—Within 7 days after the claim has

been taken possession of in accordance with the By-laws, the applicant shall sign and lodge with the Registrar for the division in which such claim is situated an application in Form 1 of By-laws.

2. *Notice of Application.*—The Registrar shall, on receipt of such application, deliver to the applicant a notice in Form 2 of By-laws.

3. *Posting Notice.*—The applicant shall, within 7 days, post, or cause such notice to be posted on some conspicuous part of the claim applied for, and keep the same there posted for 7 consecutive days, and shall, at the time of posting such notice, endorse thereon the date and time of posting the same.

4. *Certificate of Registration.*—At the expiration of such last-mentioned 7 days, if no objection against registration has been lodged with the registrar, he shall, at the request of the applicant, register the said claim in Form 3 of By-laws and shall deliver to the applicant a copy of the certificate of registration.

5. *"Survey."*—Survey of a claim shall not be necessary. If a survey is desired, and application made to a mining surveyor, he shall make a survey and fix, or cause to be fixed, at each angle of the said claim a post as prescribed hereunder.

By-law No. 4.—*Ordinary Quartz Claim.*

A holder of a miner's right, or a number of persons (not exceeding 8), each being the holder of a miner's right, and acting in conjunction, may take possession of a claim on a quartz reef not exceeding 100 feet along the line, or supposed line, of reef for every such holder. Width of claim, 600 feet.

By-law No. 5.—*Quartz Prospecting Claim.*

A holder of a miner's right desiring to prospect on or for a quartz reef may take possession of a claim of 400 feet along the line or supposed line of reef. Two persons, each the holder of a miner's right, may take possession of a claim of 600 feet along the line or supposed line of reef; such claim shall not be within 1,500 feet of any other occupied quartz claim on the same line of reef. Width of claim, 600 feet.

By-law No. 6.—Quartz Prospecting Area.

A holder of a miner's right desiring to prospect or search for auriferous quartz reefs at not less than 2 miles from the nearest occupied quartz claim may take possession of a parcel of Crown lands not more than 1,500 feet square, and provisionally occupy the same as a quartz prospecting area for a period of not more than 12 calendar months;

Or until the discovery of an auriferous lode or quartz reef therein if the latter event sooner occur.

One or more men to be kept constantly employed thereon.

Such prospecting area shall not contain within its boundaries any ground in which payable alluvial gold is known to exist.

Upon the discovery of gold in payable quantities, provisional occupation shall cease.

In lieu thereof, the said holder may take possession of a claim on the course of the reef 800 feet in length by 600 feet in width.

A person provisionally taking possession of a quartz prospecting area shall keep posted on some conspicuous place near to the prospecting bore, trench, shaft, drive, or cutting, a copy of the certificate of registration of such area.

No suspension of labour will be permitted during provisional occupation.

By-law No. 8.—Alluvial Claim.

A holder of a miner's right, or a number of persons each the holder of a miner's right, may take possession of an alluvial claim.

There shall be—

(a) An ordinary alluvial claim in new ground.
(b) A claim in old or abandoned ground.
(c) A claim in banks and bed of a river or creek.
(d) A bank sluicing claim.
(e) An ordinary puddling and sluicing claim.
(f) An extended claim for puddling, sluicing, or cement crushing.
(g) An alluvial claim in tunnelling ground.
(h) An extended claim in old and abandoned tunnelling ground.
(i) An extended claim in deep sinking.
(j) An alluvial prospecting claim.

An alluvial claim shall, where practicable, be in a square or rectangular block. Length shall not be more than three times the width, except as otherwise provided in these By-laws.

1. *Ordinary Alluvial Claim in New Ground.*—Mining in new ground shall be divided into shallow and deep sinking.

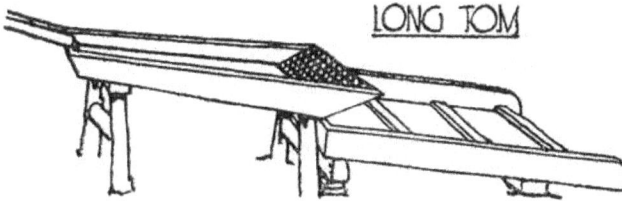

LONG TOM

Shallow sinking shall mean all shafts less than 40 feet in depth. The extent of ground in shallow sinking for each holder of a miner's right shall not exceed 75 feet in length by 100 feet in width.

Deep sinking shall mean all shafts exceeding 40 feet, and not exceeding 150 feet in depth.

The extent of ground in deep sinking for each holder of a miner's right shall be:—

(a) Where the depth of sinking exceeds 40 feet, but does not exceed 75 feet—100 feet in length by 150 feet in width.

(b) Where the depth of sinking exceeds 75 feet, but does not exceed 100 feet—125 feet in length by 200 feet in width.

(c) Where the depth of sinking exceeds 100 feet, but does not exceed 150 feet—200 feet in length by 250 feet in width.

2. *Claim in Old or Abandoned Ground.*—A claim may be taken possession of in old or abandoned ground not exceeding 150 feet by 150 feet for each holder of a miner's right.

3. *Claim on Bank or in Bed of River.*—A claim may be taken possession of on the bank or in the bed of a river or creek, not exceeding 150 feet in length by 300 feet in width, for each holder of a miner's right.

4. *Bank Sluicing Claim.*—Possession may be taken of a bank sluicing claim, that is, an alluvial claim which does not include the bed of a river or creek, not exceeding 75 feet in width by 390 feet in length for each holder of a miner's right.

5. *Puddling Claim.*—A puddling claim of not more than one acre may be taken possession of in old or partially-worked ground, or in new ground where the average depth from the surface does not exceed 10 feet, and where steam, horse or water power shall be used in puddling.

6. *Extended Claim for Puddling, etc.*—A holder of a miner's right desiring to re-work auriferous alluvial ground which has been previously worked and abandoned, and where a preliminary expense of not less than £100 is necessary for timbering or machinery or for making or cutting a race, may take possession of not more than 5 acres. A claim shall be liable to forfeiture unless the conditions herein be complied with within three months from the date of taking possession of such claim.

.   .   .   .   .   .

10. *Alluvial Prospecting Claim.*—A holder of a miner's right, prospecting for alluvial gold deposits, may take possession of and occupy provisionally as an alluvial prospecting claim until the discovery of payable gold or until such claim has been forfeited or abandoned, as follows:—

If at a distance of 1 mile and under 3 miles from the nearest occupied alluvial claim, or from any prospecting claim at the time occupied, 600 feet by 600 feet; if 3 miles and under 10 miles, 800 feet by 800 feet; if 10 miles and upwards, 1000 feet by 1000 feet. A person provisionally occupying such prospecting claim shall keep posted on some conspicuous place near to the prospecting bore, shaft, drive, trench, or cutting, a copy of the certificate of registration of such prospecting claim.

Upon the discovery of payable gold within such prospecting claim, the title to provisional occupation shall cease, and in lieu thereof the holder may take possession of as an alluvial prospecting claim double the area he might hold under the ordinary provisions of these By-laws. He shall at the time of application for registration of claim leave with the Registrar a notice in writing in duplicate, containing a full description of the locality in which the discovery has been made, the nature of the workings, and the distance of such workings from the nearest occupied alluvial claim. The Registrar shall forthwith post one of such duplicate notices in a conspicuous place at his office. A prospector failing to comply with the provisions as to registration and notice shall forfeit all benefit arising from this By-law.

By-law No. 10.—Water Right, Etc.

Definition.—For the purposes following, a water right means the right to cut, construct, and use a race, drain, dam and reservoir, and to take, divert, collect and store water.

A holder of a miner's right may, for mining purposes, cut, construct, and use a race, drain and reservoir through and upon Crown land, and may take or divert water from a stream, lake, pool, spring, creek or natural water-course situated on or flowing through or adjoining Crown land.

He may collect and store water falling upon and running through or over Crown land, and may use such water for mining purposes and for his domestic purposes.

1. *Taking Possession.*—A holder of a miner's right may take possession of a water right by placing at each end of a proposed race, and at intervals of not more than 300 feet along, or as nearly as practicable along the proposed course of the race, or at each angle of the dam or reservoir, a post as prescribed under By-law 3, and shall, within 7 days after taking possession, make application in writing to the Registrar for registration of such water right.

2. *Application for Registration.*—Application shall be in Form 4 of By-laws and shall be signed by the applicant.

A holder of a miner's right may extend his race or water-course or tail-race beyond the point for which he was originally registered, or make any alteration or deviation therein, provided that no such extension or alteration shall interfere with any registered right obtained by any other miner or miners prior to such alteration or extension. An applicant for such alteration or extension shall comply with this By-law.

3. *Notice of Application.*—The Registrar to whom application is made shall thereupon deliver to the applicant a notice in Form 5.

4. *Posting Notice and Registration.*—The applicant shall, within 7 days, post, or cause such notice to be posted on some conspicuous place on the race, drain, or reservoir

applied for, and shall keep the same there posted for 7 consecutive days, and shall, at the time of posting such notice, endorse thereon the date and hour of posting the same.

At the expiration of such last-mentioned 7 days, if there be no objection lodged, the Registrar shall register the water right and deliver to the applicant a certificate in Form 6.

5. *Quantity of Water.*—A holder of a miner's right may use a quantity of water in any one race not exceeding—

For ordinary claims, one half sluice-head;
For box-sluicing, one sluice-head;*
For ground sluicing, two sluice-heads; and
For hydraulic sluicing, three sluice-heads.

Where there is an excess of water at the head of a race, such holder may divert the same, or portion thereof, if it does not interfere with the right of any other party then existing or subsequently obtained.

.   .   .   .   .   .

12. *Width of Ground for Protection of Race.*—A holder of a race or tail-race for the conveyance of water for mining purposes shall be entitled to a width of 6 feet on each side of the race, measuring from the centre thereof. Where the depth of a cutting exceeds 8 feet, or where a tunnel is used, the width shall be 12 feet on each side of the race, measuring from the centre thereof.

.   .   .   .   .   .

32. *Tail-race.*—A holder of a miner's right may, in connection with a claim held by him, take possession of a site for a tail-race necessary for his requirements, not more than 2 miles in length, by a width of 27 feet for a distance of 60 feet from the upper end of such tail race, and a width of 12 feet for the remaining portion thereof.

33. *Taking Possession of a Tail-race.*—A tail-race shall be taken possession of in the same manner as a race under clause 1 of this By-law. The applicant for such tail-race shall, within 7 days after taking possession, make application to the Registrar in Form 12.

34. *Notice of Application.*—The Registrar to whom such application is made shall thereupon deliver to the applicant a notice in Form 13.

*Sluicehead equals one cubic foot per second.

35. *Posting Notice and Registration.*—The said applicant shall, within 7 days from the date of such last-mentioned notice, post or cause to be posted, the said notice in some conspicuous place on the course of the tail-race, and shall keep the said notice there posted for 7 consecutive days, and shall, at the time of such posting, endorse thereon the date and hour at which the same was posted. At the expiration of the said last-mentioned 7 days, if there be no objection lodged, the Registrar shall register the same, and shall deliver to the applicant a certificate in Form 14.

36. *Tailings Dam.*—A holder of a miner's right may take possession of not more than 1 acre for a tailings dam or sludge dam, into which the tailings or sludge from his claim shall run.

37. *Registration of Tailings Dam.*—A tailings dam or sludge dam shall be taken possession of and registered in the manner provided by clauses 26, 27 and 28 of this By-law.

38. *Drain for Sludge.*—Subject to the provisions of the *Mines Act* 1928, or any Act amending the same, a holder of a sluicing claim or race shall cut a drain to carry off his tailings, sludge or water, into some main channel. If, by neglecting to observe this provision, he injures a claim or gold workings, or does injury to the public, such holder shall be liable to the penalty incurred for breach of these By-laws.

39. *Nature of Embankment, Etc.*—An embankment, dam or reservoir shall be well and substantially built of solid earthwork, with a by-wash to prevent the breaking of such embankment, dam or reservoir through floods or excessive rain.

40. *Disposing of Sludge.*—A person shall not cause or permit sludge, tailings, or water to accumulate or to flow from his claim, dam or machine, so as to cause injury to a public or private road, footpath, or thoroughfare;

Or to a claim, drive, water-race, water-dam, water-hole for domestic purposes, or old or new workings;

Or to a puddling machine or other machinery;

Or to a garden or place of residence held by any other person under miner's right or business licence.

By-law No. 19.—*Objection.*

1. *To Registration.*—A person objecting to the registration, protection or suspension of a claim or tenement shall, within 7 days from the date of the posting of the notice of application for registration, protection or suspension, as provided under the By-laws, lodge with the Registrar a notice in Form 38 of By-laws. The Registrar shall, on receipt of such notice, defer the registration, protection or suspension of such claim or tenement until a Warden has heard and adjudged the matter of the objection, or until default has taken place, as provided in this By-law.

2. *Prosecution.*—A person so objecting shall, within 7 days after lodging such notice, cause to be issued by a Warden a summons to the person applying for registration, protection, or suspension requiring him to appear before a Warden to have the matter of such objection heard and determined.

3. *Failure to Prosecute.*—Should a person so objecting fail to cause a summons to be issued, as provided in this By-law, such objection shall be null and void, and the Registrar shall complete such registration, protection or suspension as if no objection had been made.

4. *Warden's Order on Hearing.*—The Warden may, on the hearing of a summons, either dismiss the same or may make an order restraining the said Registrar from proceeding further with such registration, protection or suspension.

By-law No. 20.—*Work in Claims.*

1. *Mode of Working.*—A holder of a claim under the By-laws, either personally or by substitute, within 14 days after registration of such claim, shall *bona fide* proceed to work, and shall, unless such claim be held under protection, continue to work regularly upon or in connection with such claim, according to the usual course of efficient mining.

FEES FOR REGISTRATION, ETC.

	s.	d.
Registration of application for claim, etc., for any number of persons, including form of application	1	0
Registration of single claim or share	0	6
Transfers, each share or interest	2	0
Certificate, each	0	6
Inspecting records, each inspection	1	0
Registration of water right, race, tail-race, drain, dam, or reservoir, each	1	0
Miners' rights	2	6

Note.—Forms of application for registration may be obtained from mining registrars.

A GLOSSARY OF SOME TERMS COMMONLY USED IN PROSPECTING AND FOSSICKING.

Alluvial. The soils, clays, sands or gravels, the result of denudation, and found usually in watercourses and on flats.

Back. The exposed roof of lode, tunnel or drive.

Bar of Ground. A layer of a harder nature usually than the enclosing strata.

Basalt. A hard rock of igneous origin.

Basin. The area drained by a river or a creek; a dry watercourse.

Bedrock. The strata (usually consisting of slates and sandstones) upon which an alluvial deposit rests.

Bottom. The bedrock.

Break. A fault or fissure in the rock formation.

Claim. A portion of ground held for working by means of a miner's right.

Color. Slight traces of gold.

Conglomerate. A mass of rocks cemented together.

Costeaning. Narrow excavations through surface soil and across the probable line of lode to expose cap.

Crab-holes. Depressions caused by subsidence or decomposition of rocks.

Cradle. See Chapter II.

Creek-claim. A claim established on the banks or in the bed of a creek.

Crevicing. Searching for gold particles in the cracks or crevices of river bars.

Cross-cut. That part of a level cut at right angles to the course of the lode or strata.

Crushing. Reduction of quartz by mechanical means.

Dolly. A pestle and mortar used for pounding samples.

Drive.	That part of a level driven on the lode.
Face.	The end of a drive; the perpendicular surface of a lode or excavation.
False-bottom.	A layer supporting a deposit of wash dirt some feet above the true bedrock.
Fault.	A displacement of the strata.
Fine Gold.	Minute fragments of gold.
Floating Reef.	Displaced or detached fragments of reefs or strata.
Flume.	The runway of sluice boxes or races.
Fossicker.	One who reopens old workings for traces of gold previously overlooked.
Ground-sluice.	A channel cut into the natural rock formation, and used instead of wooden sluices.
Gutter.	Synonymous with alluvial lead.
Hopper.	In a cradle, the sieve or perforated top.
Deep Lead.	A deep alluvial gutter. A deposit beneath several layers of newer sand or gravel or rock.
Level.	Embraces crosscut and drive.
Loaming.	The process of tracking to their source the detached portions of a lode (see Chapter II).
Lode.	A fissure filled with quartz or other minerals.
Miner's Right.	A document which permits the holder to take possession of Crown lands under the mining by-laws.
Mullock.	The country rock derived from developmental work.
Nugget.	A lump of gold.
Open Cutting.	A quarry.
Ore.	Metal or mineral with accompanying gangue that may be worked profitably.
Pan.	A shallow sheet iron dish.
Panning Off.	The process of washing by means of the pan.

Prospect.	A show of gold in a dish or in the exposed face of a lode.
Prospector.	One who searches for minerals with a view to their further development by mining.
Puddling Machine.	A machine for washing large quantities of gravel to eliminate clay, rubble, etc.
Quartz.	A hard, glassy mineral in which gold may occur.
Race.	A canal or artificial waterway.
Reef.	Lode or vein; the slate or sandstone bedrock of an alluvial lead.
Reef Wash.	Wash dirt adjacent to the lead lodged on the reef or bedrock at a higher level.
Riddle.	A sieve used to divide gravel and stones from the finer silt.
Riffle.	Small wooden bars placed in cradles and sluices to retain fragments of gold.
Rise.	An opening from a lower to an upper level, usually on the lode.
Seam.	A horizontal layer.
Seepage.	Slow passage of water through drifts or other strata.
Shoot of Ore.	A continuous body of payable ore in the lode.
Tailings.	The waste material dumped after treatment operations.
Tail-race.	An artificial canal to convey discharged water or tailings.
Trenching.	Shallow excavations on line of lode to test outcrop or cap of lode.
Wash-dirt or Wash.	Auriferous gravel, sand or clay.
Winze.	An opening from an upper to a lower level, usually on the lode.

Brown, Prior & Co. Pty. Ltd., 430 Little Bourke St., Melbourne, C.1.

GLOSSARY

ACID ROCKS.- Igneous rocks containing a high percentage of silica.

AMPHIBOLITE.- A metamorphic, in places schistose, rock, with hornblende as the chief constituent and with subordinate felspar.

ANTICLINE.- An arch-like fold of strata having a long axis so as to form a ridge instead of a dome.

ASBESTOS.- A general name given to a number of fibrous non-combustible silicate minerals, usually white, grey or greenish grey in colour. The chief varieties are chrysotile, crocidolite (blue asbestos) and anthophyllite. The fibres should be easily separable, strong, fine and silky.

BASALT.- Usually a fine-grained basic igneous rock which has been cooled on the surface of the earth as a lava flow. A basalt, however, may never reach the surface before cooling.

BASIC ROCKS.- Igneous rocks containing a comparatively low percentage of silica.

BAUXITE.- Aluminous laterite. Ferric oxide, silica and titanium oxide are present in varying amounts. Used in the production of aluminium.

BERYL.- Silicate of beryllium and aluminium. Colour various, may be green, blue, yellow, grey or white. Often found as well crystallised hexagonal prisms. Sometimes shows striations due to parallel growth. When showing no signs of crystallisation, it is difficult to distinguish from quartz. Flawless transparent crystals are valued as gem stones. Chief ore of beryllium.

BISMUTITE.- A basic carbonate of bismuth of variable composition. Cream colour; earthy. Ore of bismuth.

BLOCK FAULTING.- The breaking and moving of large portions of the earth's crust, by which distinct blocks of varying height are formed.

"BLOWS."- A local term applied to prominent hills of quartz and ironston.

BREAKAWAYS.- A local term applied to the steep cliffs connecting old and new plateaux. The top of the cliff is usually capped by laterite, below which the rocks are decomposed.

BRECCIA.- A rock composed of angular fragments of pre-existing rocks, consolidated by some cementing material, such as silica, carbonate of lime, etc. The constituent rock fragments may be formed by the ordinary agents of weathering or by the crushing force exerted by great earth movements.

CASSITERITE (Tinstone).- Oxide of tin. Heavy (specific gravity, 6.9). Commonly found in river gravels as black pebbles.

CEMENT.- A local term indicating a tough rock which in some places is "wash" cemented together by silica or other material, and in other places is decomposed bedrock hardened by the same material.

CHALCOPYRITE (Copper Pyrites).- Sulphide of copper and iron. Colour, brass yellow. Surface tarnishes readily, sometimes becoming irridescent, when it is known as peacock ore.

CHERT.- A common typo of chalcedony, which is a form of oxide of silicon.

CLAY.- A general name for the fine aluminous sediments that are plastic.

CONGLOMERATE.- A rock composed of pebbles rounded by water action or by earth movements, nod cemented by ferruginous, calcareous silicious or other material.

COSTEANING.- Says the Century Dictionary: "The general direction of the lode having been, us supposed, approximately ascertained by means of work already done, the object of the costeaning is to trace the lode still further through ground where its outcrop is not visible on the surface." This is not the Australian interpretation. If the lode is believed to run North and South the costean usually takes the form of a trench running East and West. It is an exploratory trench whose width and length are determined by the circumstances.

CROCOITE.- Chromate of lead. Colour, various shades of red. Soft. A minor constituent of some ores. Being heavy and bright, has been mistaken for gold by prospectors when panning.

DEEP LEADS.- As used in Western Australia, this term means old stream channels, which have become so buried beneath the waste of the land that the channels no longer act as drainage lines.

DEFORMATION.- The folding, fracturing, faulting and warping of the earth's crust by earth movement.

DIABASE.- A basic igneous rock frequently occurring in sheets or dykes. Broadly speaking, it may be called an altered dolerite. One of the "greenstones."

DOLERITE.- A dark coloured basic igneous rock consisting largely of augite and felspar. One of the "greenstones."

DOLOMITE.- A rock of mineral consisting of carbonate of lime and magnesia.

DYKES.- Bands of generally vertical or nearly vertical igneous rocks, which traverse other rocks and which are thin in proportion to their length and depth.

EPIDIORITE.- An altered "greenstone" rock now consisting of hornblende and felspar.

FAULT.- A fracture in the earth's crust, along which one or both of the adjacent rock masses has or have moved.

FAULT PLANE.- The surface along which the rock masses have moved during the formation of a fault.

FELDSPAR- Group name. Silicates of aluminium with varying amounts of lime, potash and soda. The chief varieties are microcline (potash feldspar), plagioclase (soda-lime feldspar) and albite (soda feldspar). All feldspars cleave easily in two directions nearly at right angles, splitting with even, smooth and shiny surfaces. Used in ceramic industry.

FLUORITE (Fluorspar).- Fluoride of calcium. A glassy mineral of many different colours. Usually well crystallised in the cubic system. Sometimes massive. Easily scratched. Used as a flux.

FOLDED ROCKS.- Rocks which, by movements within the earth's crust, have been thrown into a series of arches and troughs of a widely varying character.

FOLIATIONS PLANES.- A series of approximately parallel close-set planes in a rock mass, by which minerals are arranged in distinct lines, and the rock acquires an appearance somewhat like the edges of a book.

GABBRO.- A basic igneous rock generally of deep-seated origin and composed of augite and felspar.

GALENA.- Sulphide of lead. Generally in blue-grey masses or cubic crystals. Soft, metallic lustre, and a perfect cubic cleavage. May carry rich silver values. The principal ore of lead.

GNEISS.- A rock generally similar in composition to a granite but having its component minerals arranged in definite layers or " folia." A gneiss is a metamorphic rock and may result from either a sedimentary or an igneous rock.

GRANITE.- A crystalline rock consisting essentially of quartz and felspar grains with any of the following minerals present in minor proportions : Biotite mica, muscovite mica, or hornblende. The Western Australian goldfields granites usually consist of quartz and felspar with some biotite mica,.

GREENSTONE.- A field term applied to more or less altered rocks which have a characteristic dark green colour due to the presence of the minerals chlorite, hornblende, epidote, etc. It may be either schistose or massive.

HAEMATITE.- Any anhydrous oxide of iron.

HAEMATITE-QUARTZITE.- A metamorphic rock commonly occurring on the goldfields of Western Australia composed chiefly of haematite and quartz. Frequently referred to as "Jaspar Bar " or "Banded Iron Formation."

HORNBLENDITE.- A rock consisting almost wholly of hornblende plates or prisms and containing no felspar.

IGNEOUS ROCKS. - Rocks which have originally been in a molten condition and have cooled either on or within the earth's crust.

JASPER.- Opaque chalcedony of red, brown, yellow or green colour. frequently applied to the Banded Iron Formations.

JOINTS.- Cracks or partings in a rock distinct from bedding or cleavage planes.

LATERITE.- A term used in Western Australia to indicate the hard cap on granite and other rocks, such cap having resulted from the decomposition of those rocks. Laterite may be predominantly ferruginous, aluminous or silicious.

LAVA.- A rock which in a molten state has issued from vents or fissures and which solidifies on· or close to the surface of the earth.

LIMESTONE.- A rock composed mainly of carbonate of lime. Most limestones have been formed in the sea by the accumulation of the hard parts of marine animals and plants.

LIMONITE.- Hydrous oxide of iron. Of widespread occurrence. Commonly brown ; massive. Colour ranges from yellow to nearly black. Ore of iron and constituent of most soils and as a brown staining en many minerals.

MANGANESE.- Manganese minerals seldom occur· singly, but usually as mixtures in association with limonite. Manganite, polianite, psilomelane and pyrolusite are all oxides of manganese; black in colour. They vary from soft and earthy to hard and massive.

Manganese oxide forms as a black stain on many minerals.

MARL.- An earthy and usually soft form of limestone.

MICA.- Group name for various silicate minerals characterised by a perfect basal cleavage whereby they readily split into thin elastic sheets. Muscovite (potash mica) and phlogopite (magnesian mica) occur in large transparent or slightly stained sheets highly valued for their electrical insulation and heat resistance properties. Lepidolite (lithia mica) is ore. of lithium. Biotite (black mica) has no commercial value.

MOLYBDENITE.- Sulphide of molybdenum. Usually as small soft bluish-black scales with a bright metallic lustre. Strong resemblance to graphite. Leaves a bluish-grey trace on paper. Ore of molybdenum.

PYRITE (Iron pyrites).- Sulphide of iron. Pale, brassy to golden yellow in colour. Usually in granular masses or grains; sometimes as well crystallised cubes. Sometimes called "new chum gold." May occasionally carry gold values. Commercial source of sulphur in the manufacture of sulphuric acid.

PYROXENITE.- A granitoid, non-felspathic rock, the chief mineral of which is pyroxene. It contains no olivine.

QUARTZ.- A common form of oxide of silicon. There are many varieties. Rock crystal is the purest form.

QUARTZ PORPHYRY.- An acid igneous rock closely related to granite, but generally found in dykes and small masses; contains round or nearly round quartz crystals up to half inch diameter.

QUARTZITES.- Metamorphic rocks formed almost wholly of silica grains. They are of various origin.

ROCK HOLLOW.- A hollow or cave cut more or less horizontally beneath a hard rock cap or at the foot of a lake cliff of hard rocks.

ROCK WEATHERING.- The general term applied to all natural methods by which a rock is broken up and decays.

SANDSTONES.- Rocks composed essentially of compacted, usually quartz, sand. The character of the rock may vary according to the cementing material, such as iron, lime, etc.

SCARP.- The face forming a sharp transition from a higher to a lower belt of country. It may be due either to erosion or faulting.

SCHEELITE.- Calcium tungstate. Colour variable, commonly white to greenish-yellow. Usually as granular masses of scattered grains. Fairly heavy (specific gravity, 6.1). Ore of tungsten.

SCHISTS.- Metamorphic rocks (with a predominant mineral such as mica, hornblende, etc.) which split along approximately parallel lines.

SEDIMENTARY ROCKS.- Rocks which have been formed as sediments or deposits under water. Wind-blown deposits (aeolian rocks). are generally included in this series, notwithstanding their inability to fit the definition. .

SHALE.- A sedimentary clayey rock, which splits along the original planes of deposition.

SHOAD.- The word "shoad," sometimes spelt "shode," means "floaters," or loose fragments of ore mixed with earth, lying on or near the surface and indicating the proximity of a lode. "Shoading" is a word in use in some mining districts and is the process of searching for valuable ore by collecting and examining loose stones on the surface or slightly buried in the soil. The expression "shed-ore" is more often heard than "shoad-ore," and more likely to be understood by the prospector.

SILL.- A sheet of volcanic rock injected between layers of other rocks.

SLATE.- A clayey rock which splits into thin plates at various angles to the bedding.

SPHALERITE (Zinc blende).- Sulphide of zinc. Colour varies, commonly brown. Generally in cleavable, fine to coarse granular or compact masses. Brittle; resinous to adamantine lustre. Chief ore of zinc.

STRATA.- The series of successive deposits one above the other which compose a sedimentary rock.

STRIKE.- The general trend or direction in a horizontal line of a lode, stratum or fault.

SYNCLINE.- A trough-shaped curve of strata, having one long axis, which distinguishes it from a basin.

TANTALITE-COLUMBITE.- The minerals of this group are tantalates and niobates of iron and manganese. They form a continuous series grading from tantalite (the iron tantalite) through mangano-tantalite (the manganese tantalite) and columbite (the iron niobate) to mangano-columbite (the manganese niobate). They are heavy black minerals, somewhat resembling cassiterite. Specific gravity varies from 7.9 tantalite to 5.2 columbite. Tantalite is the chief ore in the production of tantalum.

URANINITE (Pitchblende).- Mainly oxide of uranium. Source of uranium and other radioactive elements. The pitchblende variety is usually black and pitch-like in appearance.

WEATHERING.- The decomposition, disintegration and breaking up of the earth's crust by the action of changes of temperature and of rain, wind and frost.

WOLFRAMITE (Wolfram).- Tungstate of iron, and manganese. Generally as thick tabular or bladed crystals. Colour usually black with, a brilliant metallic lustre. Heavy (specific gravity, 7.4). Ore of tungsten.

This Glossary first appeared in *Hints to Prospectors* by Hugh Corbet first published in 1932.

HINTS TO PROSPECTORS

This book was written by Hugh Corbet, Deputy Master of the Perth Mint, published in 1932, and sought to gain interest in larger forms of gold production. This book includes the results from the last edition which shows the results for 1958 in Western Australia, areas still rich for the grey nomad or professional prospector; and a section pertaining to the process of dry-blowing, "a method adopted in Western Australia for freeing pounded gold ore from the powdered matter when water is not available."

The book includes much practical information, including: taking & preparing samples for assay; recovery & cleaning gold amalgam from battery; hints for and care of battery; methods of cyanidation; miners' rights; prospecting hints for the new man; use of explosives; first aid and more.

Hints to
Prospectors

Hugh Corbet

IMPRINT
CLASSICS

PROSPECTOR'S GUIDE : Victoria

A Grey Nomad Guide from the 1930s

This book was prepared by George Brown for the Victorian Department of Mines in 1932, and sought to gain public interest in local prospecting. Sections include Working Alluvial Deposits, the Geological formations of Victoria, Gold Deposits, Quartz Reefs, the Ballarat Indicators, and detailed notes on gold finds throughout Victoria; areas still rich for the grey nomad or professional prospector. The book includes much practical information on Miner's Rights, By-Laws and Leases.

Now in Imprint Classics, 98 pages facsimile.

Prospector's Guide : Victoria

A Grey Nomad Guide from the 1930s

IMPRINT CLASSICS

PROSPECTING FOR GOLD

'I felt certain there must be gold in those hills, Jack', wrote a prospector to Ion Idriess, 'but I know very little about the game.' And so Jack Idriess wrote Prospecting for Gold in 1931. This is the 20th edition and known throughout Australia as the classic self-help manual for would-be prospectors.

'This book is written to help the new hand who ventures into the bush seeking gold... The "towny" prospector, with this book as a guide, will soon master methods of prospecting and the working of his find.'
In an easy conversational tone, the author of Lasseter's Last Ride and Flynn of the Inland sets many a hopeful prospector on the road to discovering gold.

Prospecting
for Gold

ION IDRIESS

IMPRINT
CLASSICS

www.ingramcontent.com/pod-product-compliance
Lightning Source LLC
Chambersburg PA
CBHW041110110426
42740CB00054B/3446